Colorful Colorado

Old Colorado City

By

Michael Robert Serovey, MA, MISM

Former US Army Sergeant

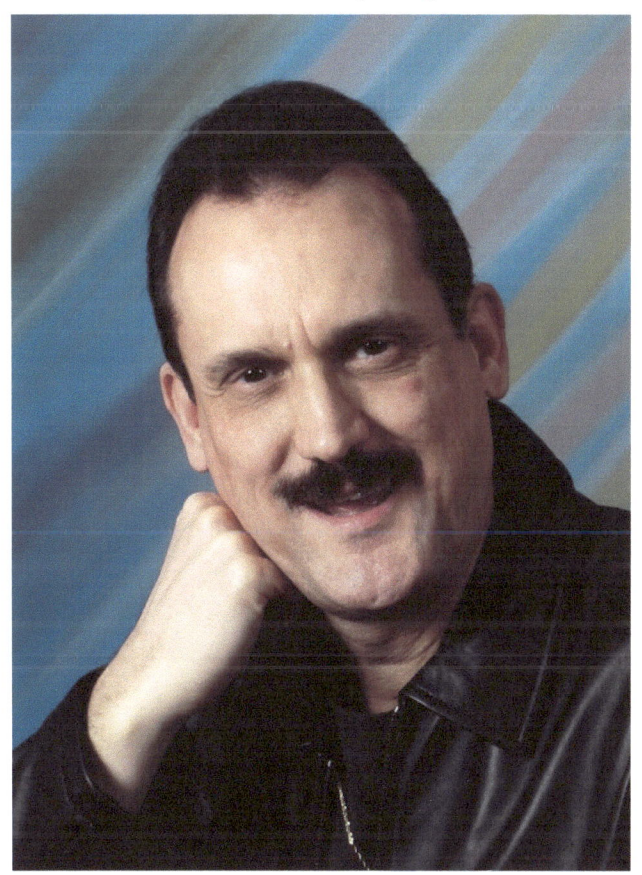

Copyright Information Page

Table of Contents

Introduction

This short book is a collection of pictures that I took of Old Colorado City, which is the original Colorado Springs, Colorado. These photographs were taken during September of 2014 when I was temporarily homeless and staying in an RV park in this area. These photographs have been edited to improve the appearance of some of them and / or to remove people and trademarks.

The Main Drag (Colorado Avenue)

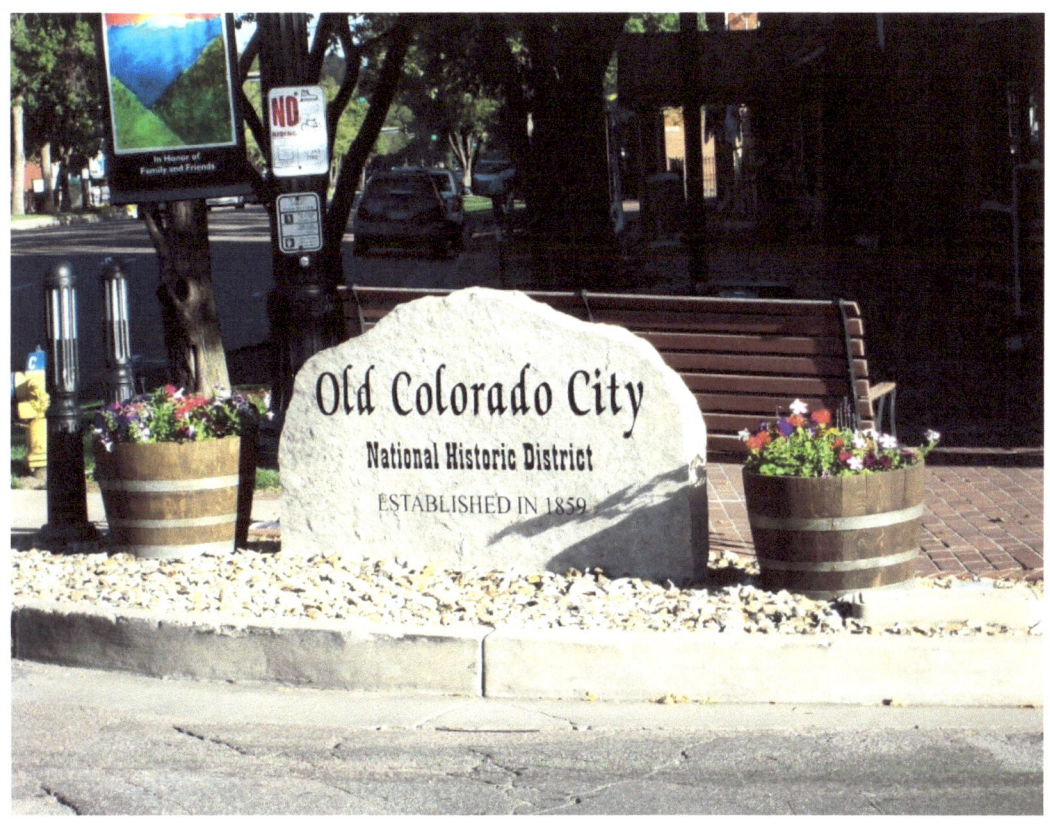

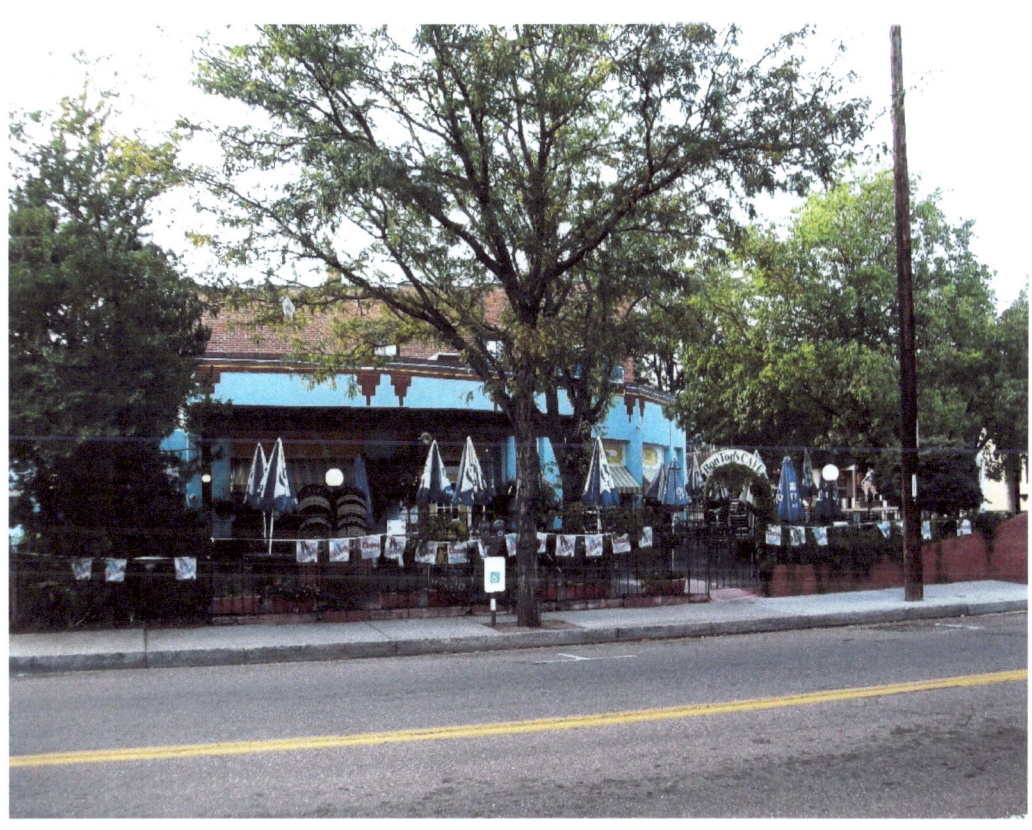

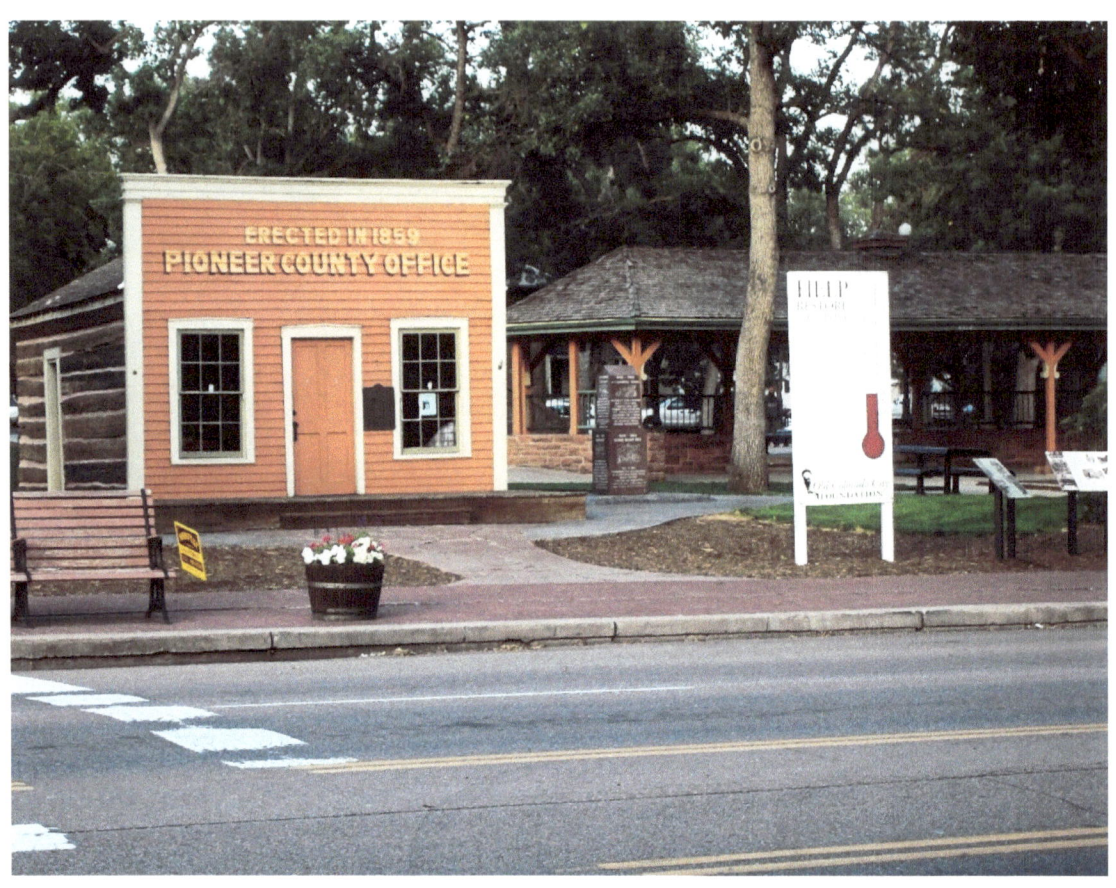

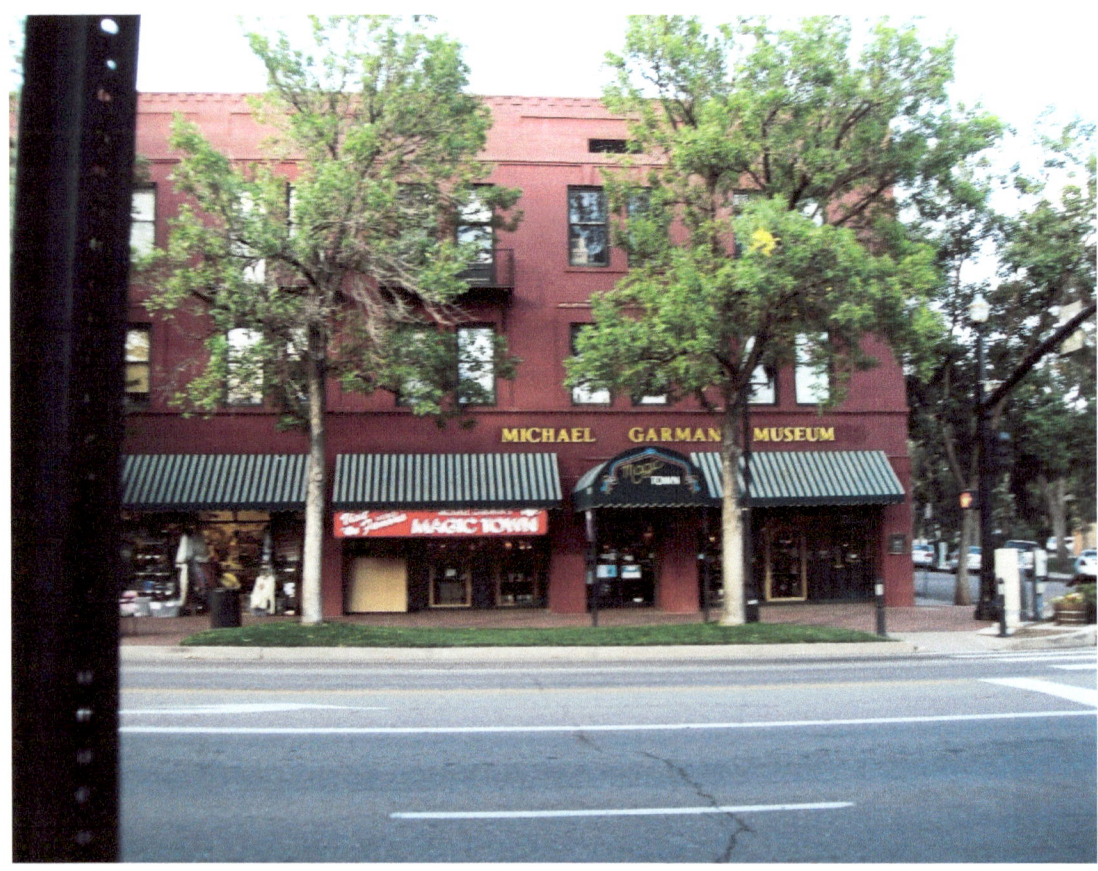

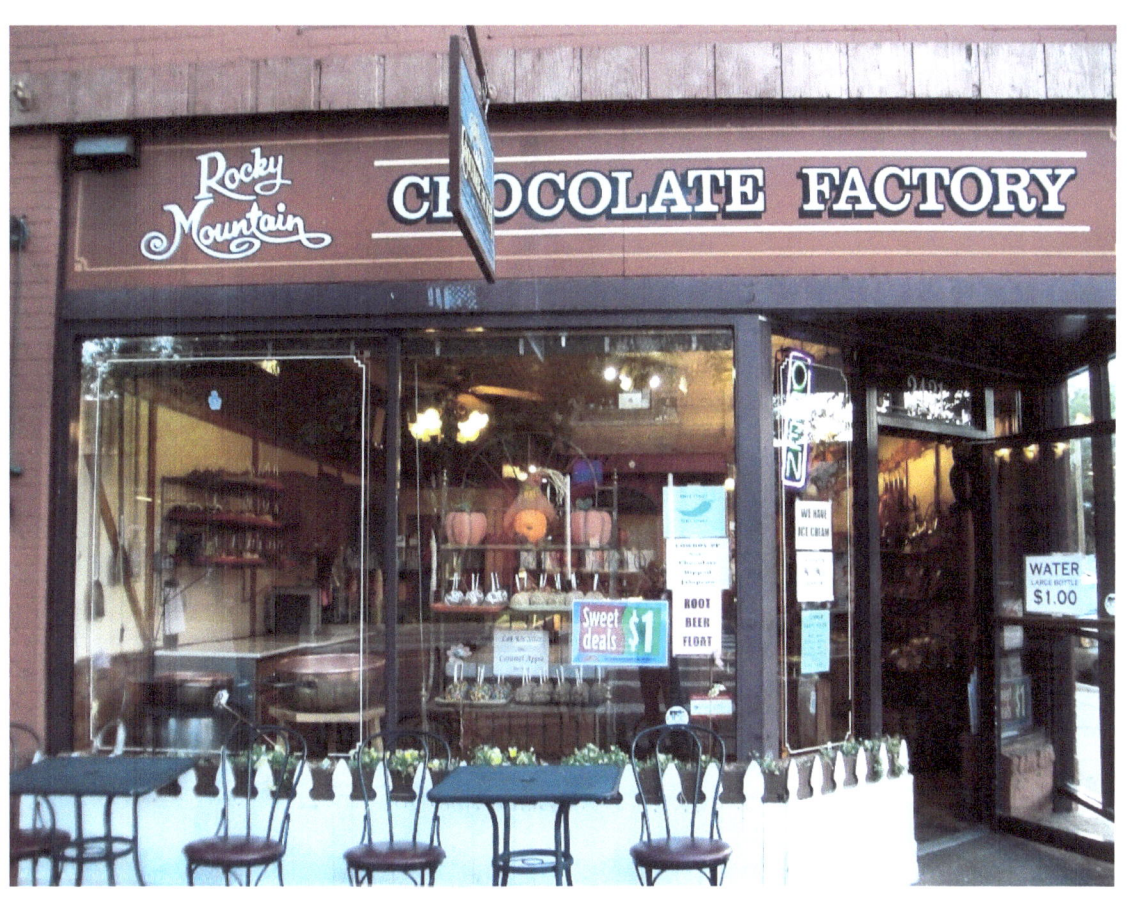

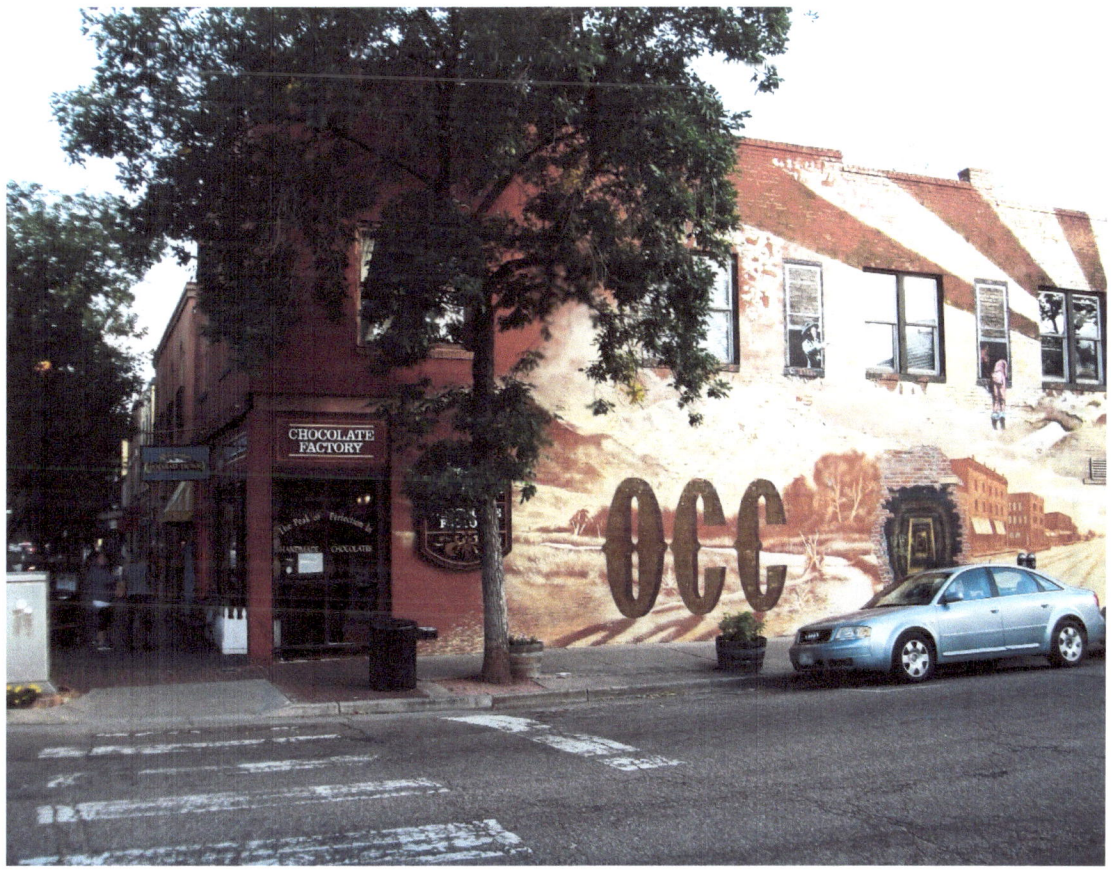

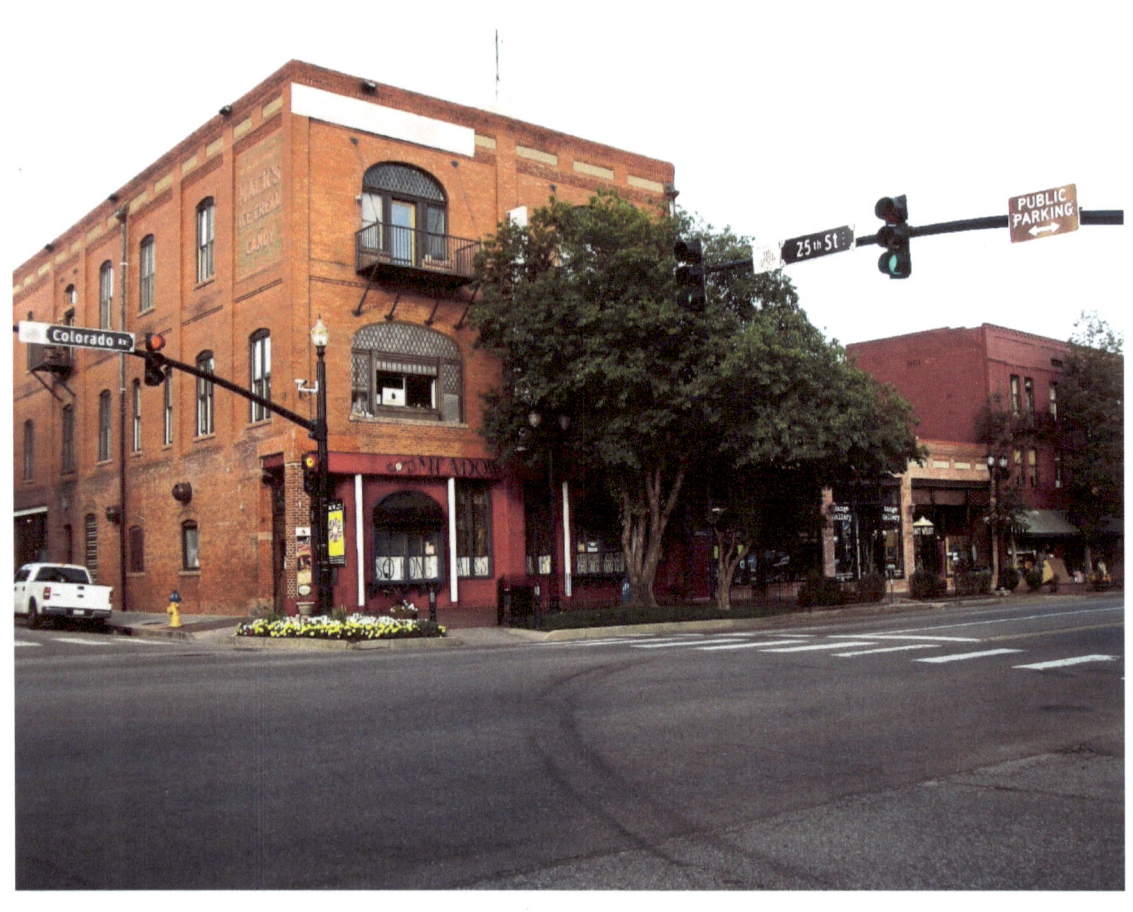

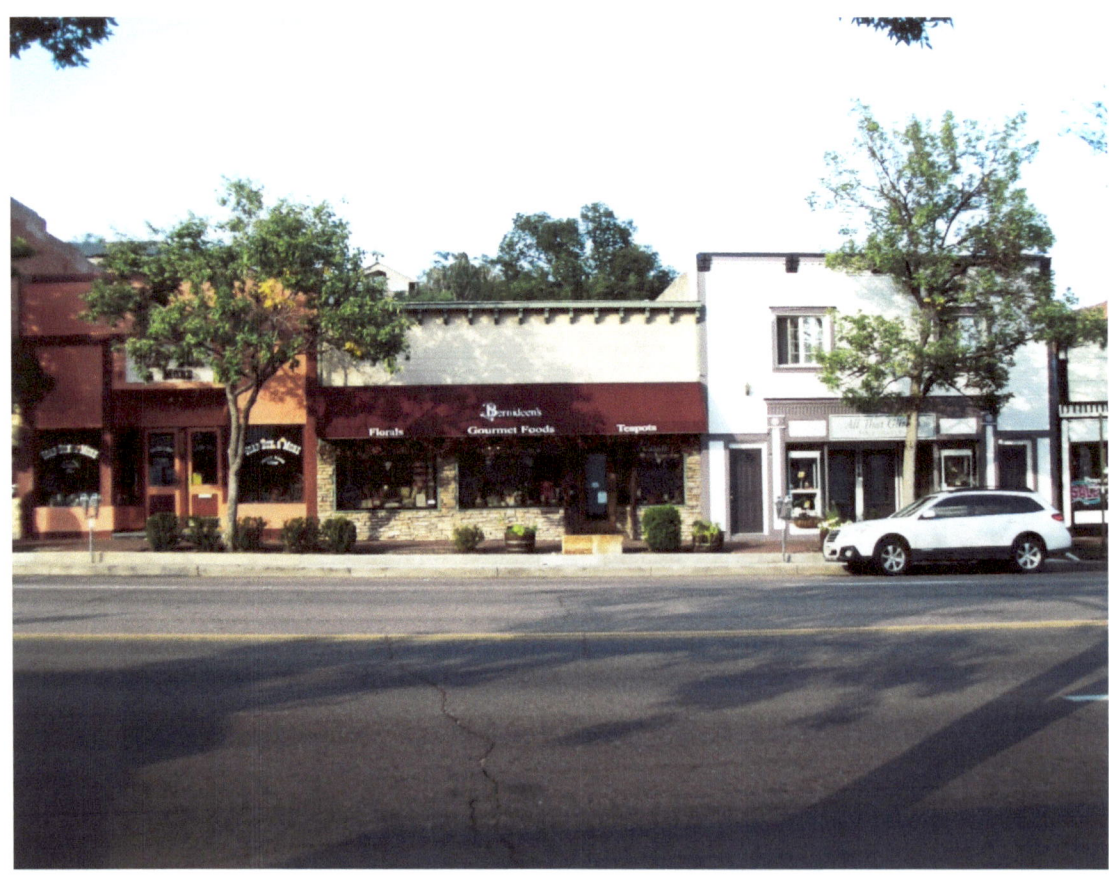

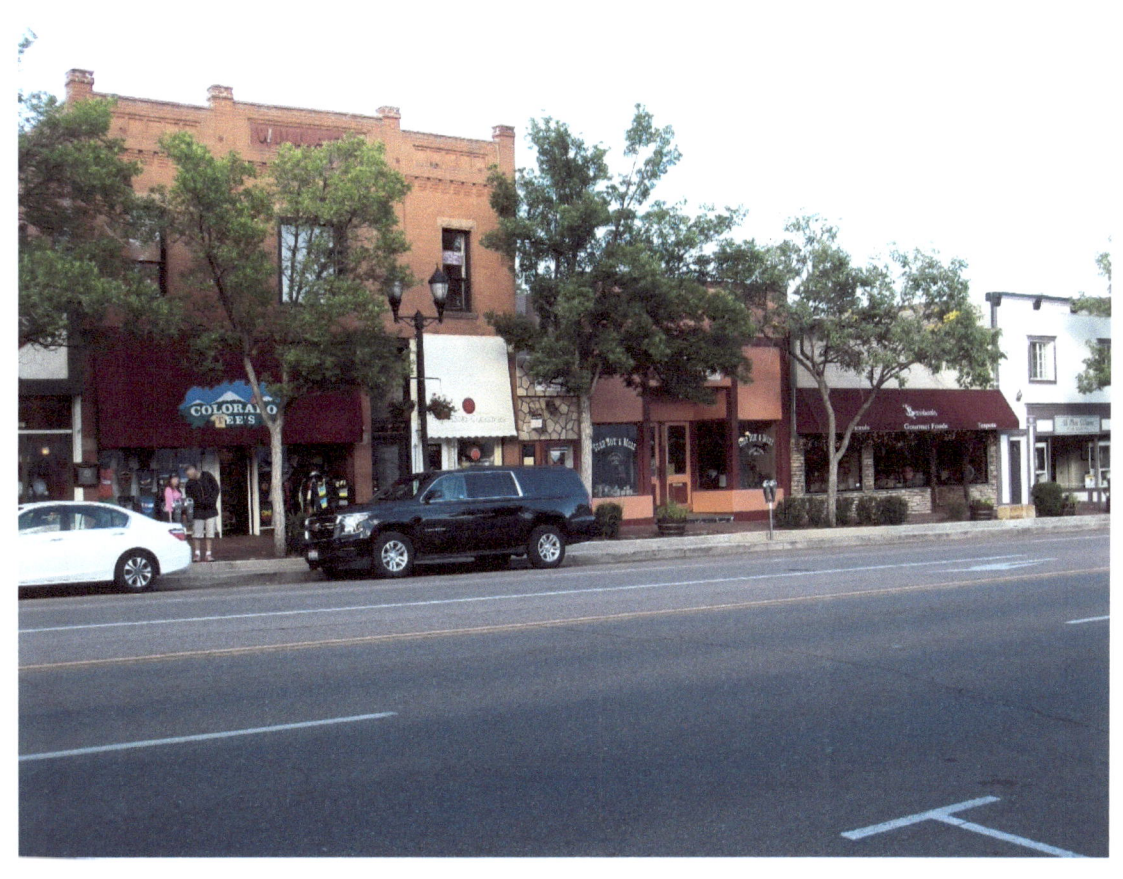

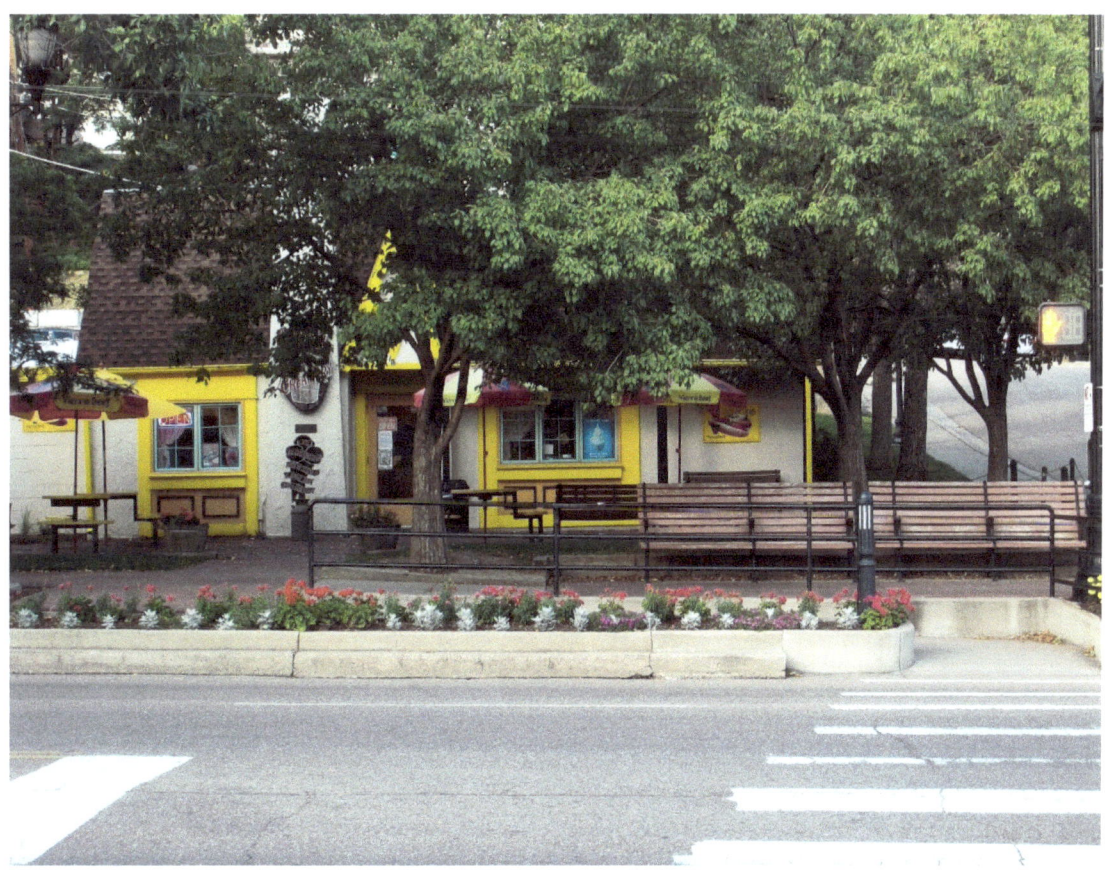

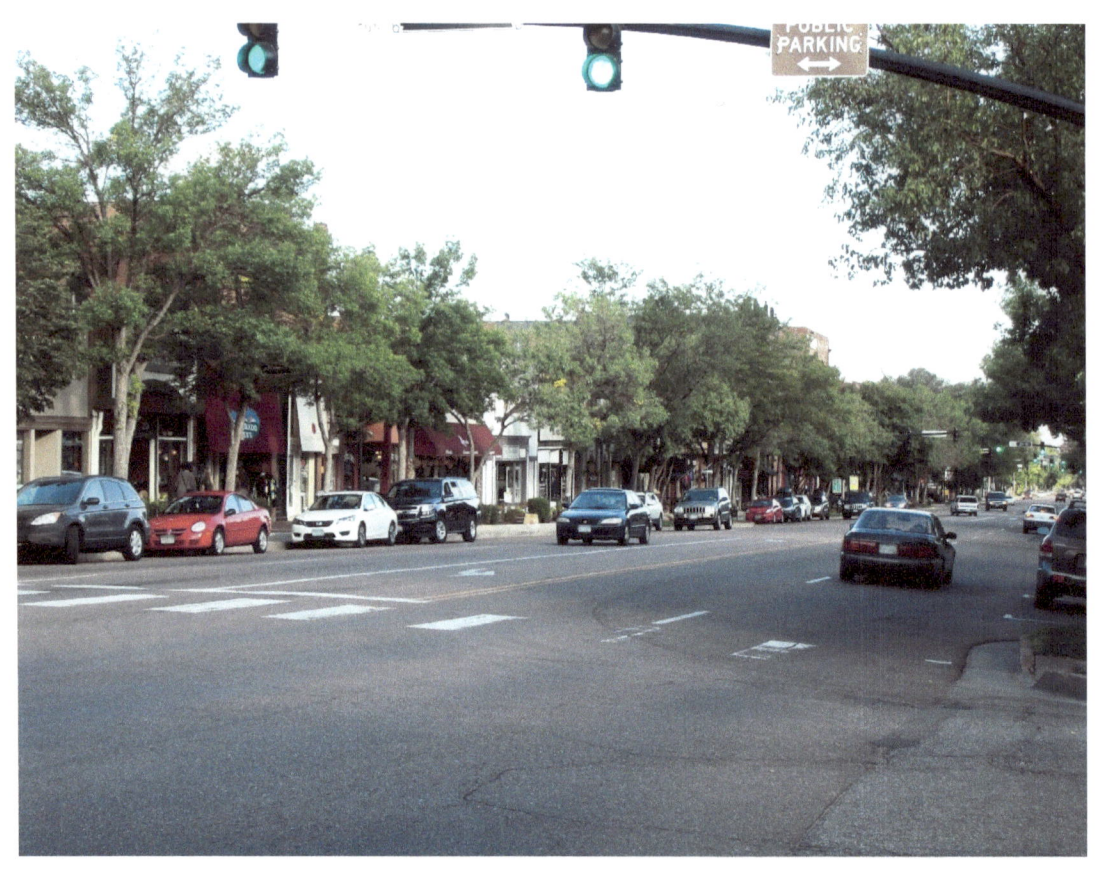

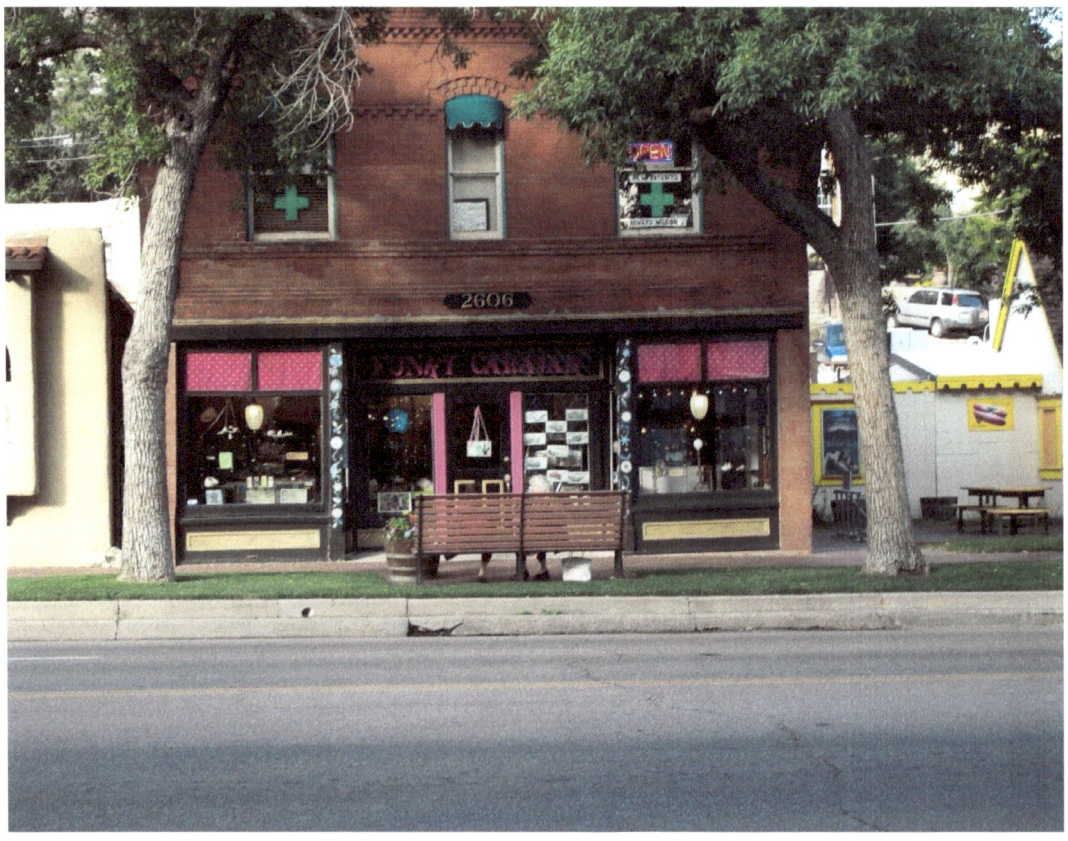

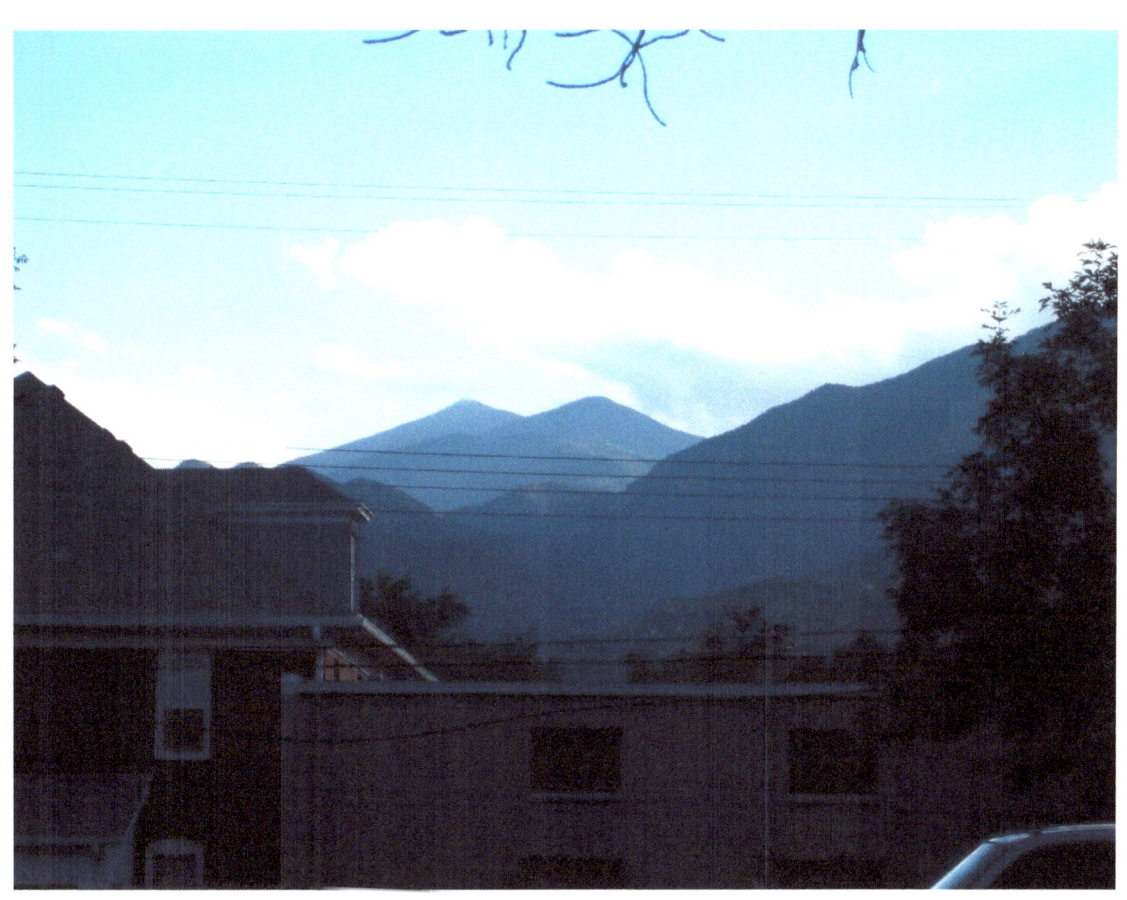

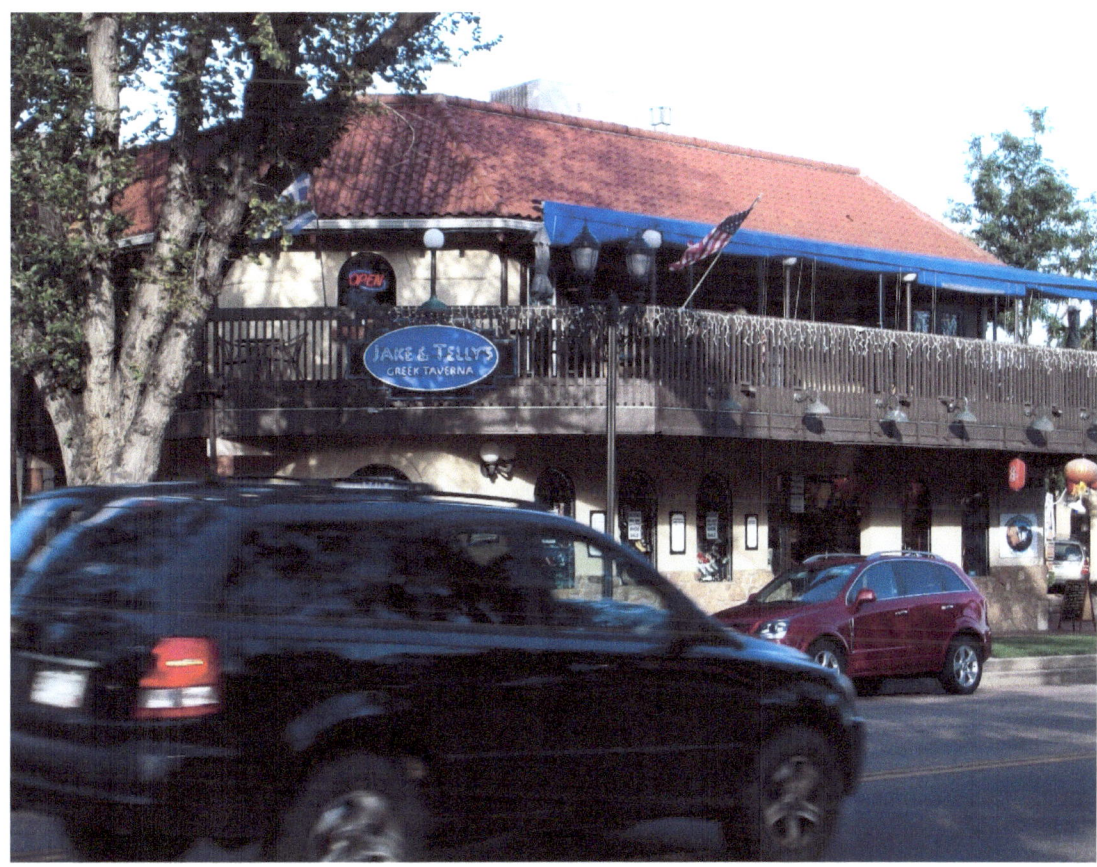

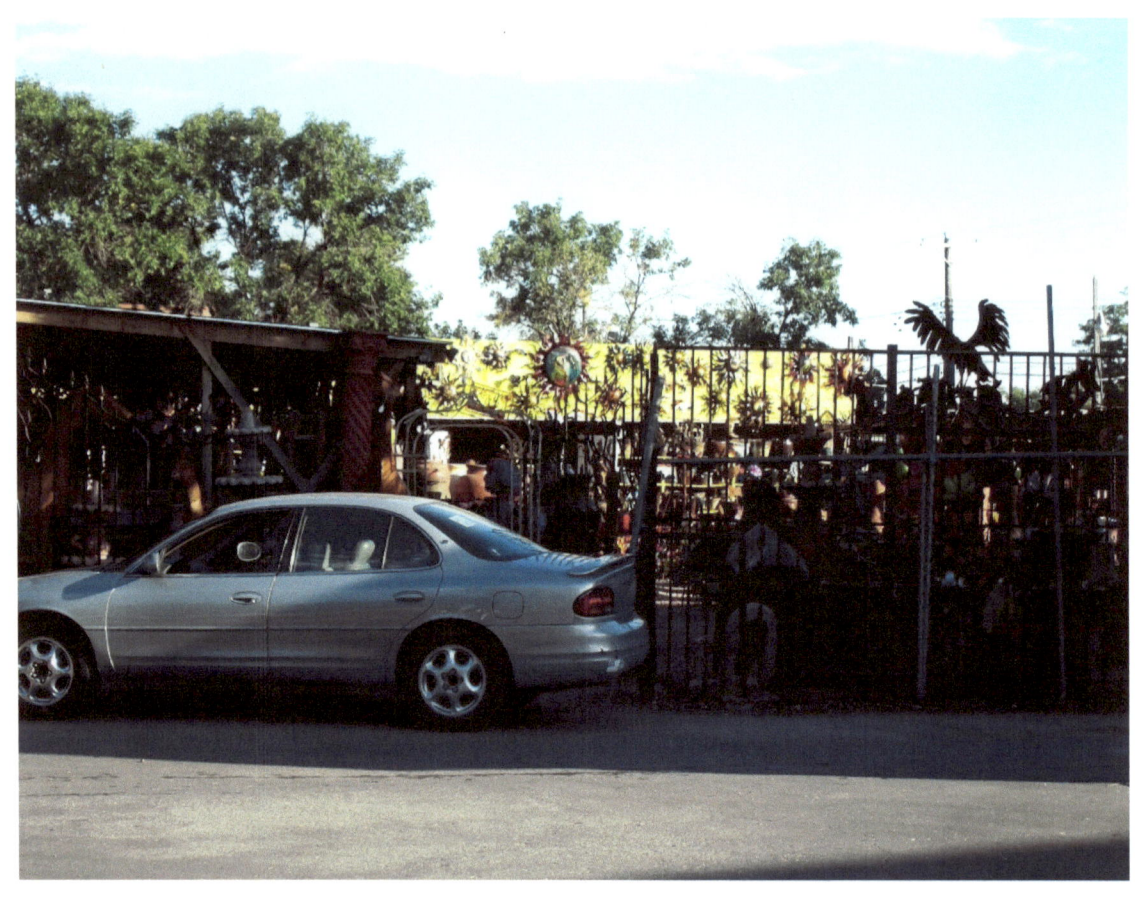

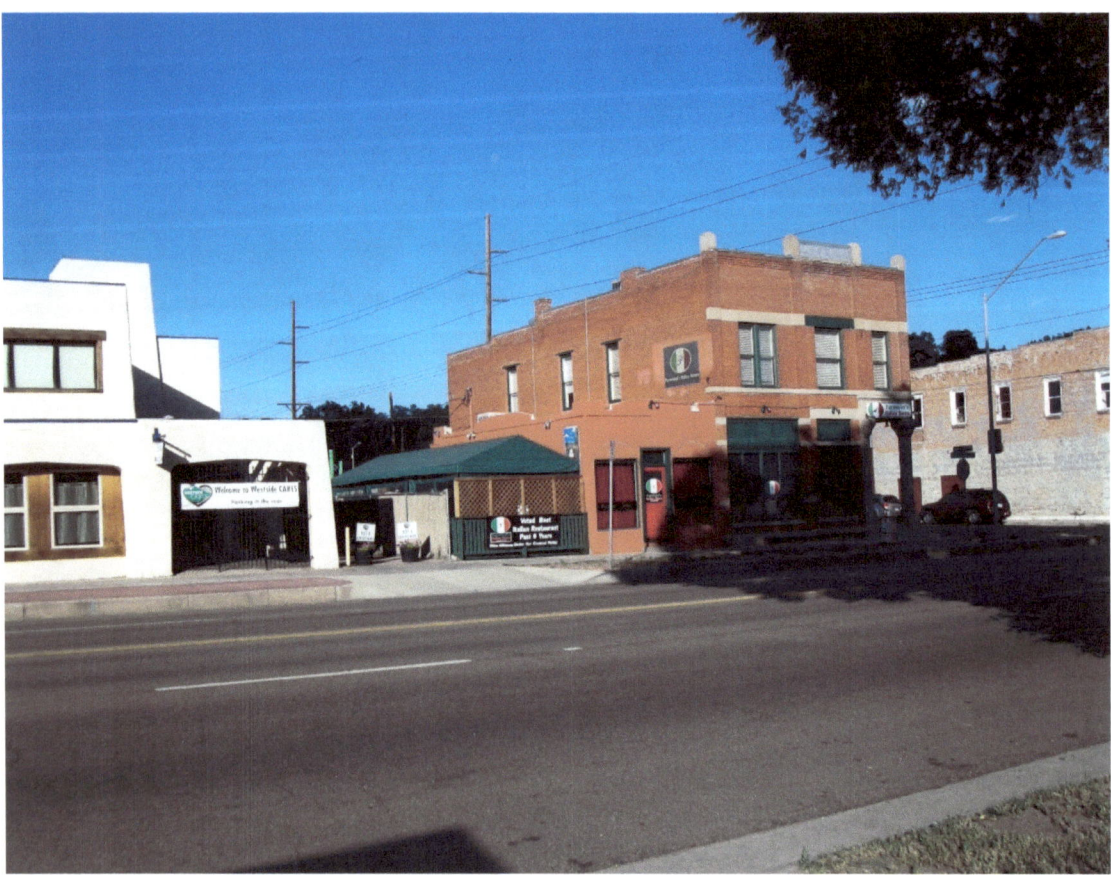

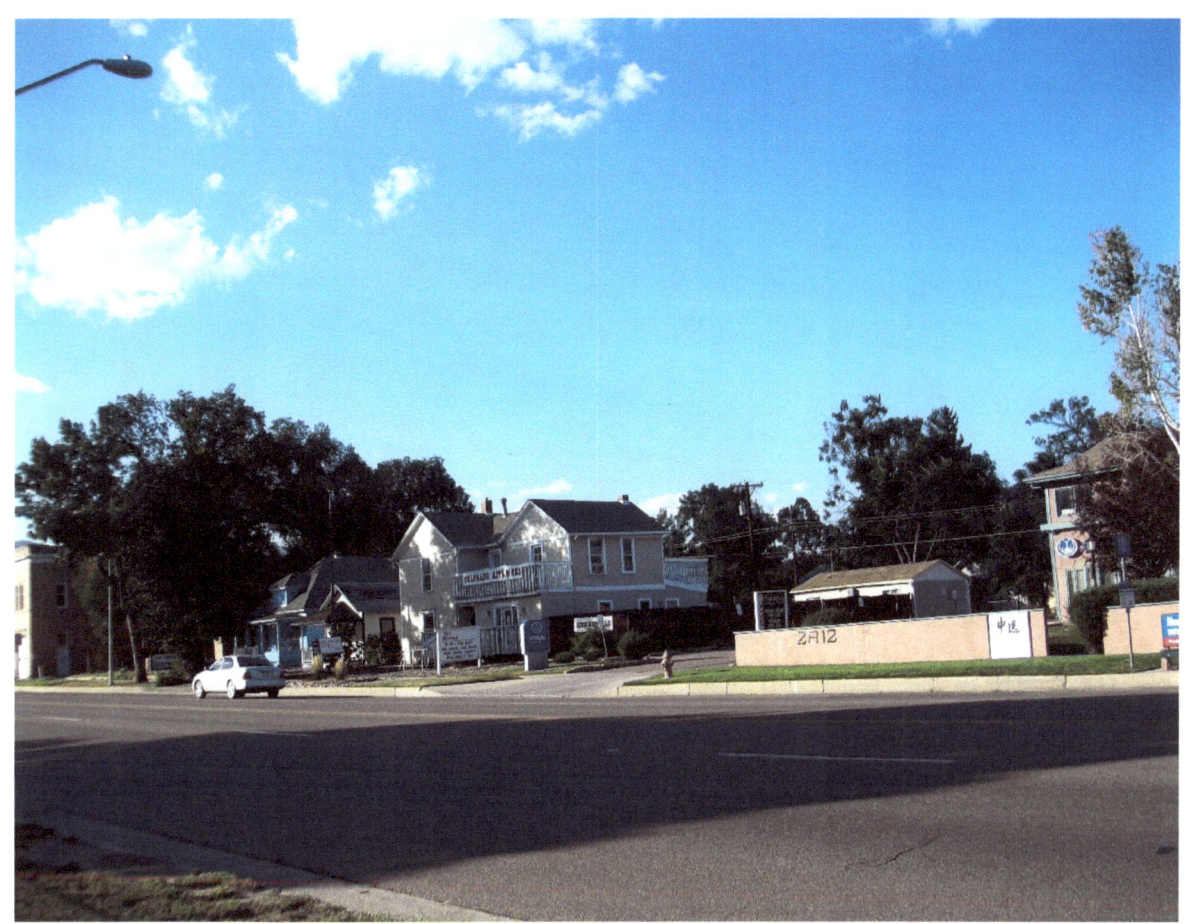

Side Streets

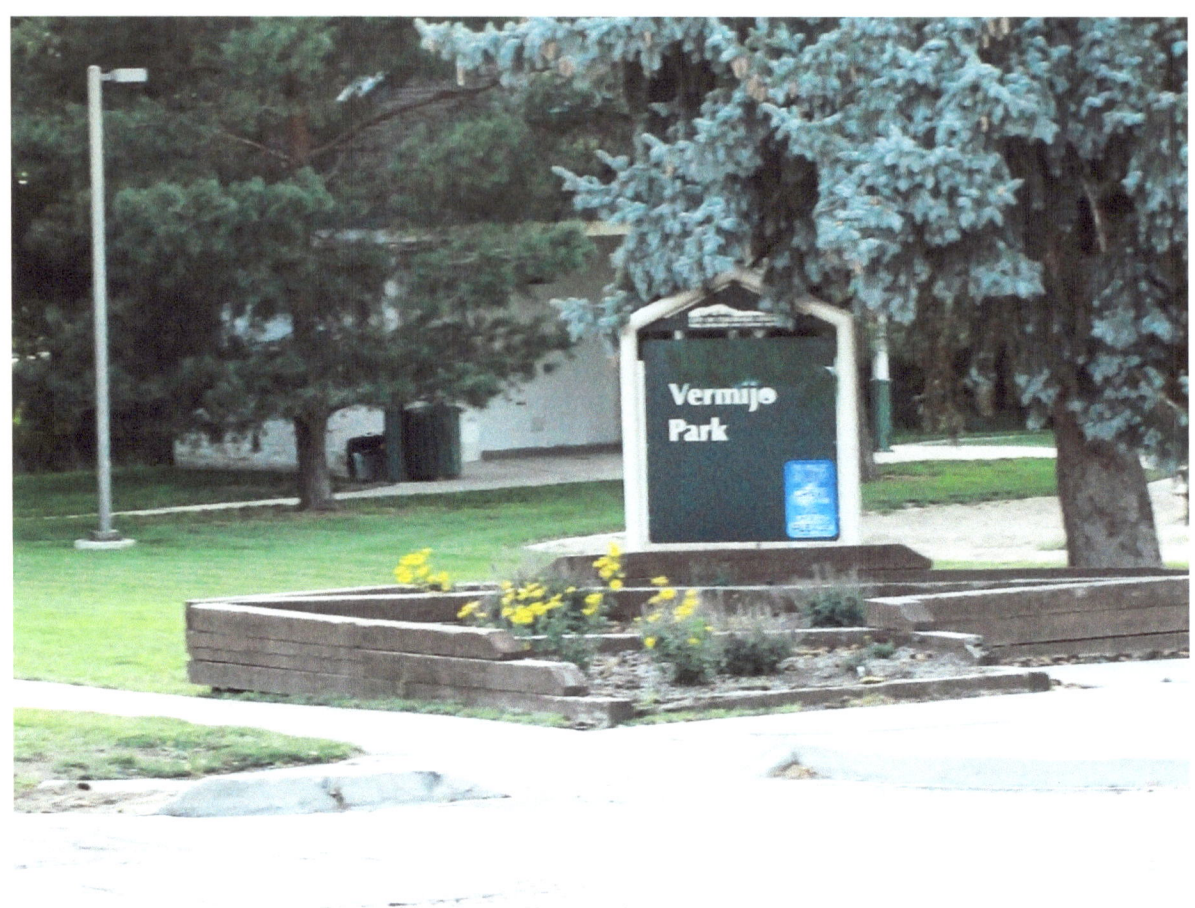

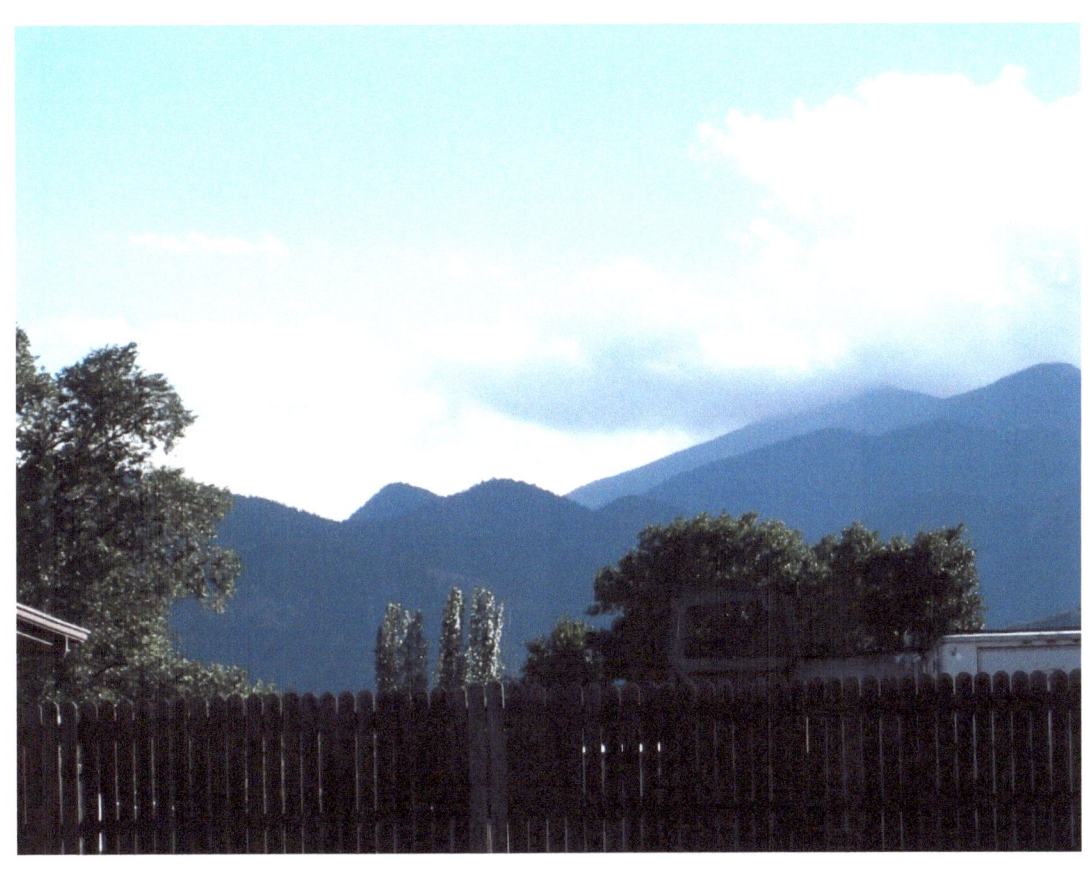

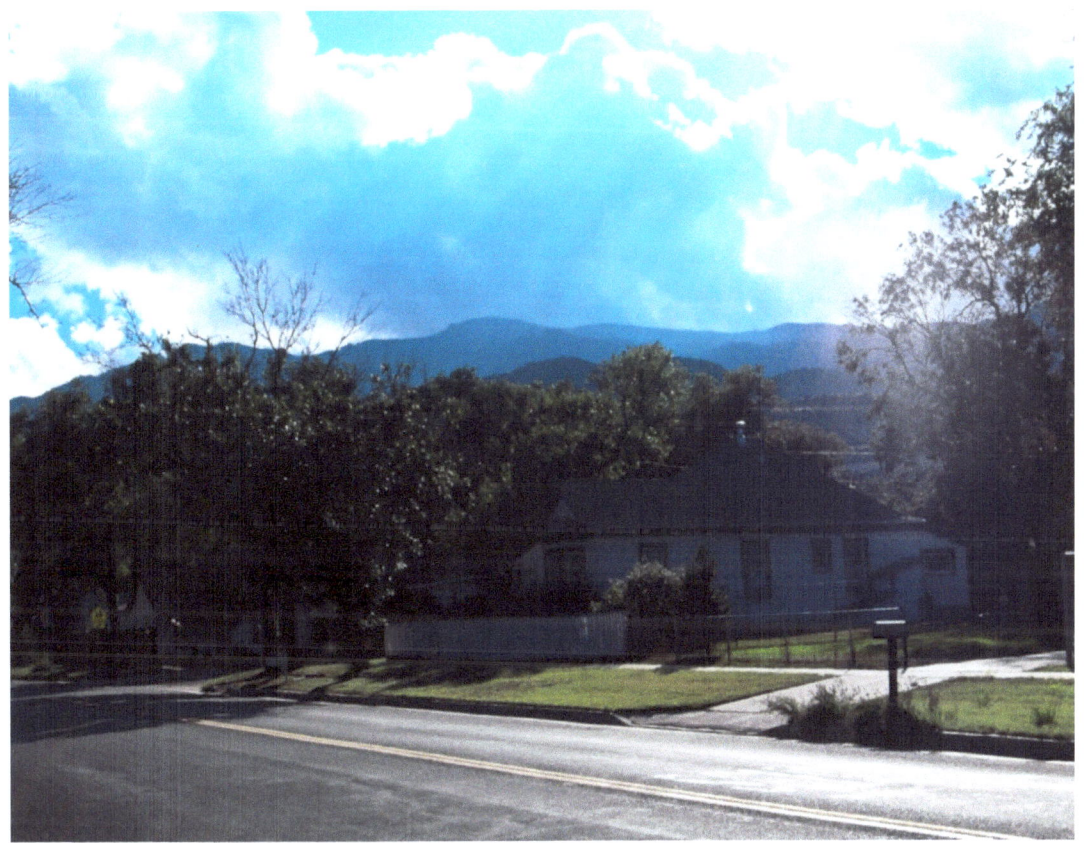

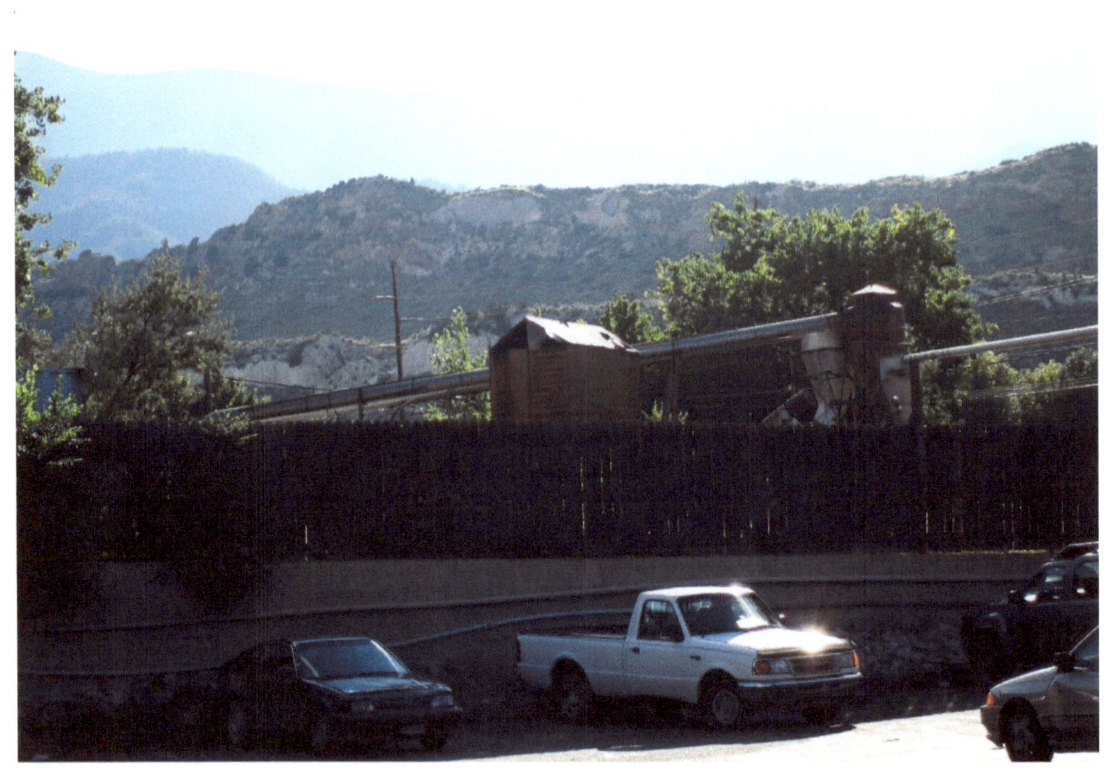

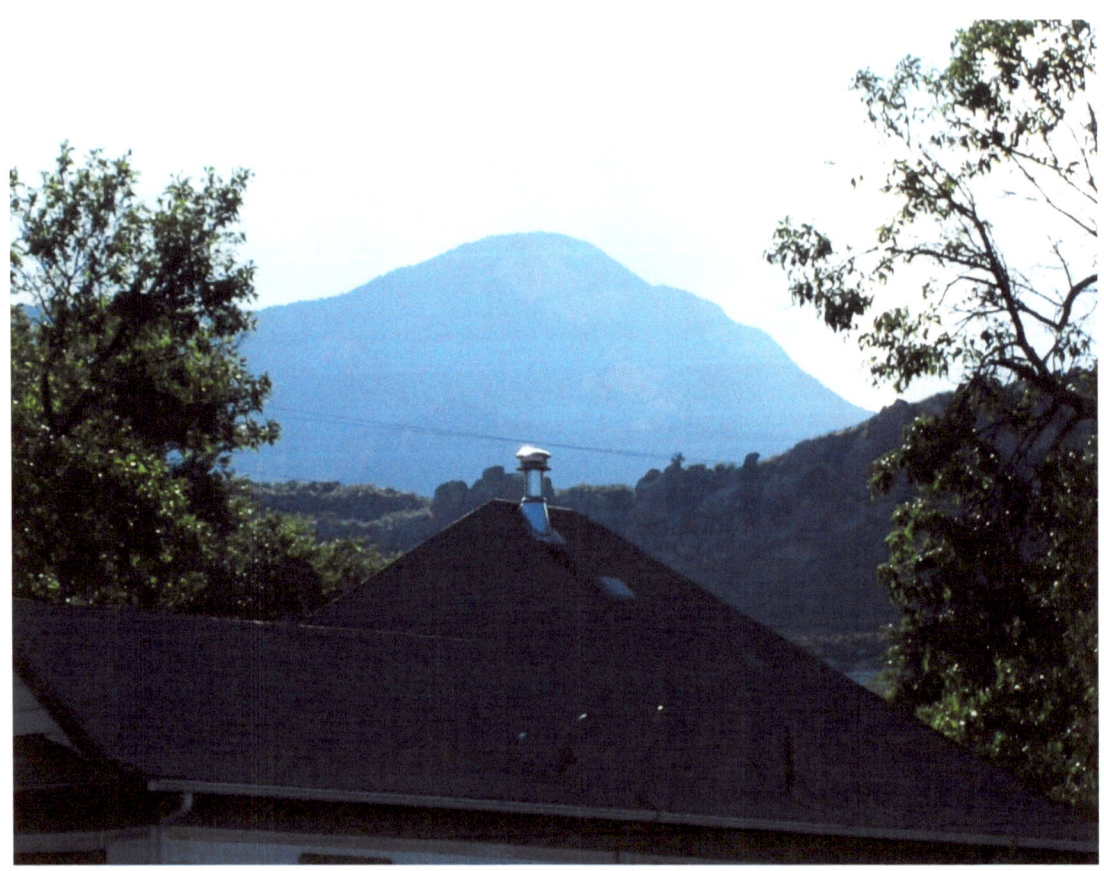

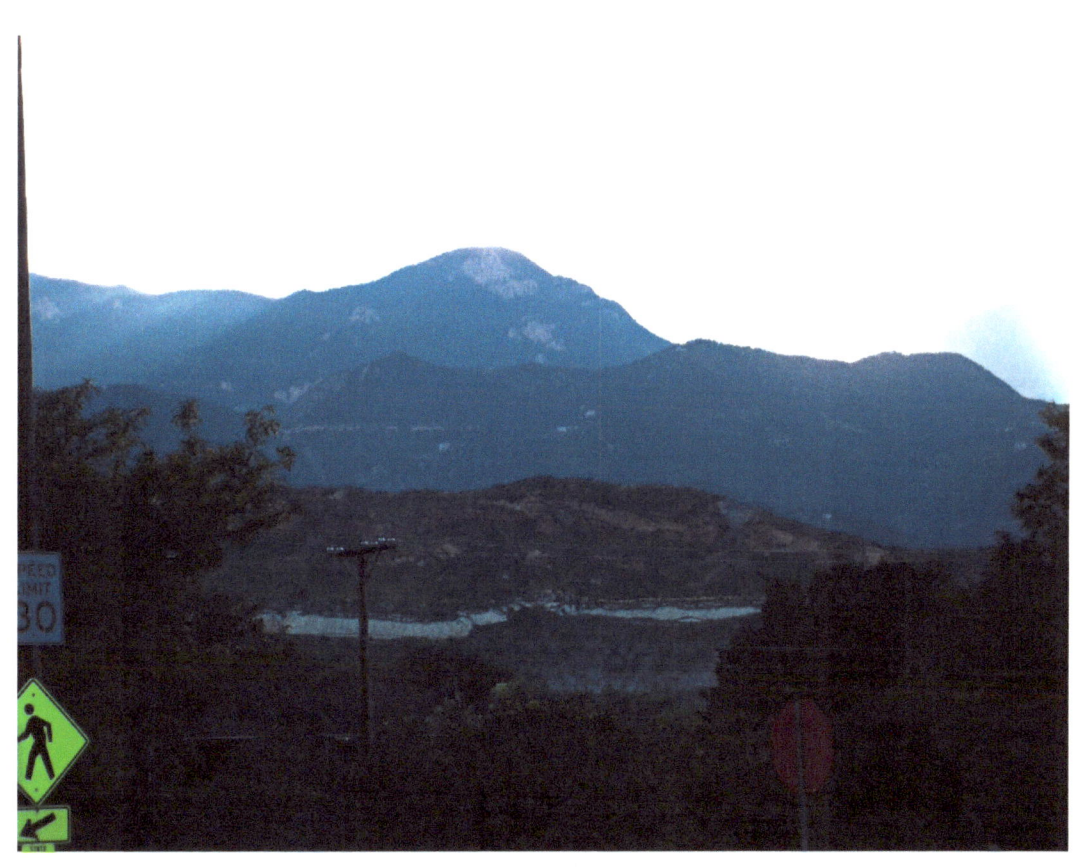

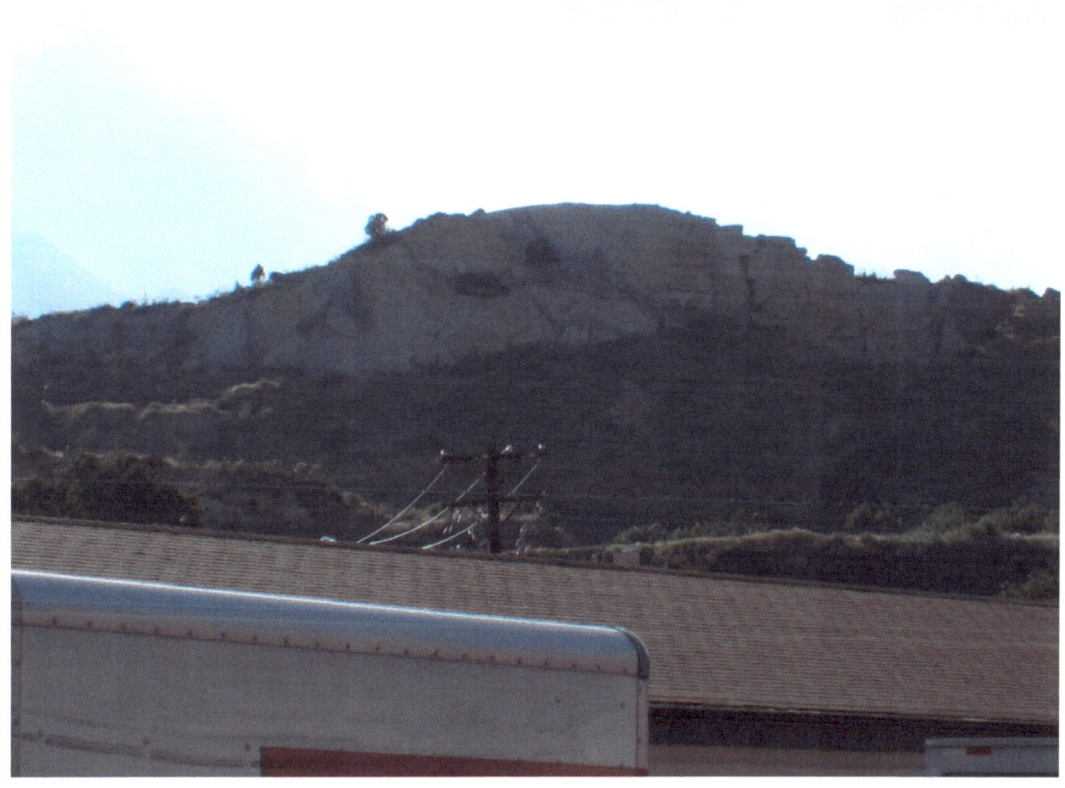

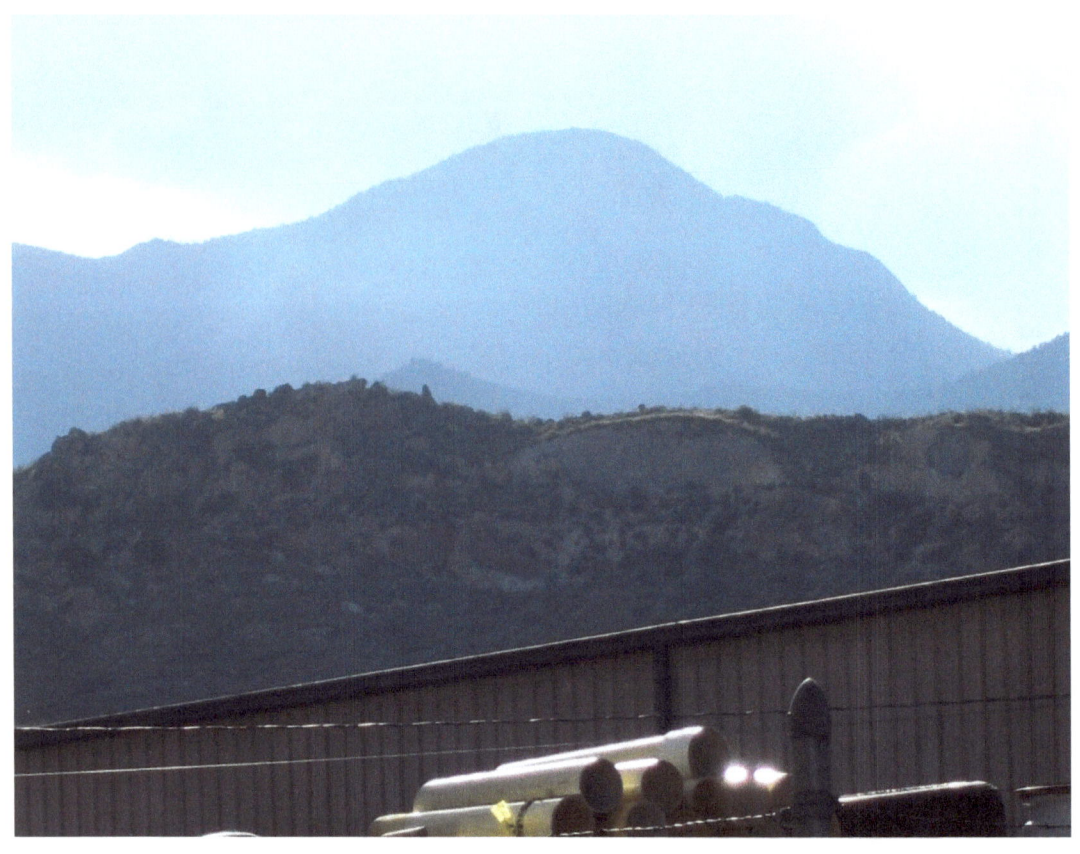

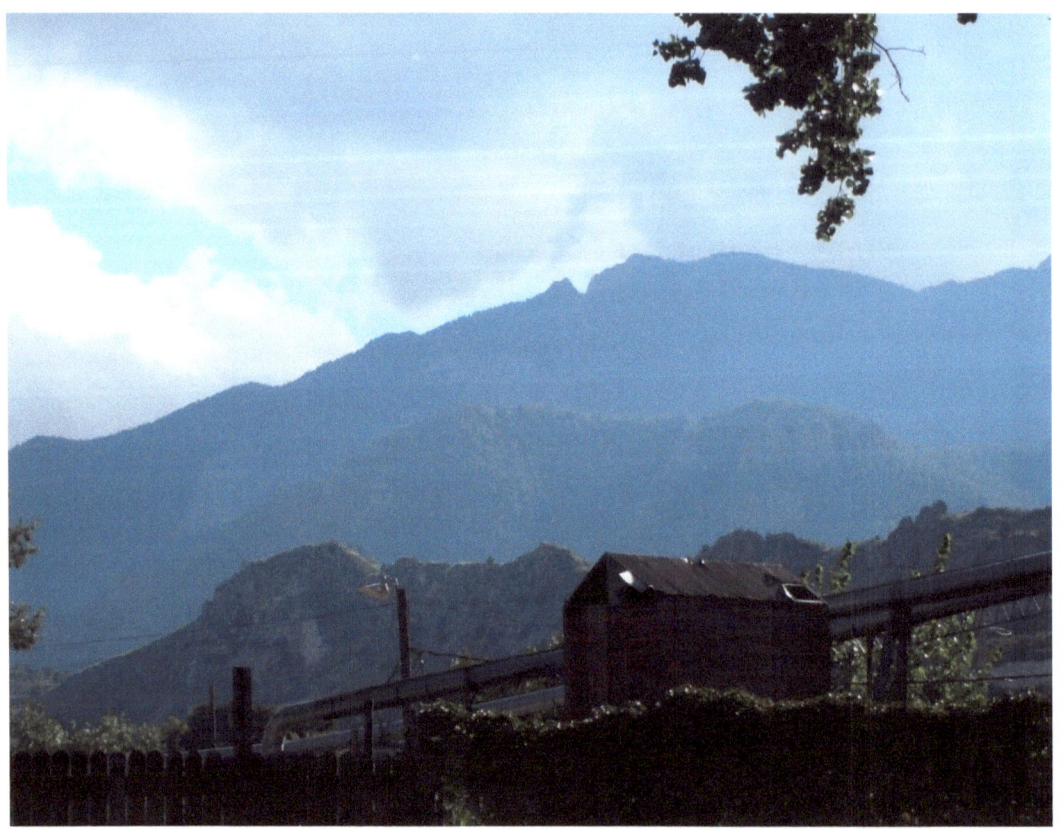

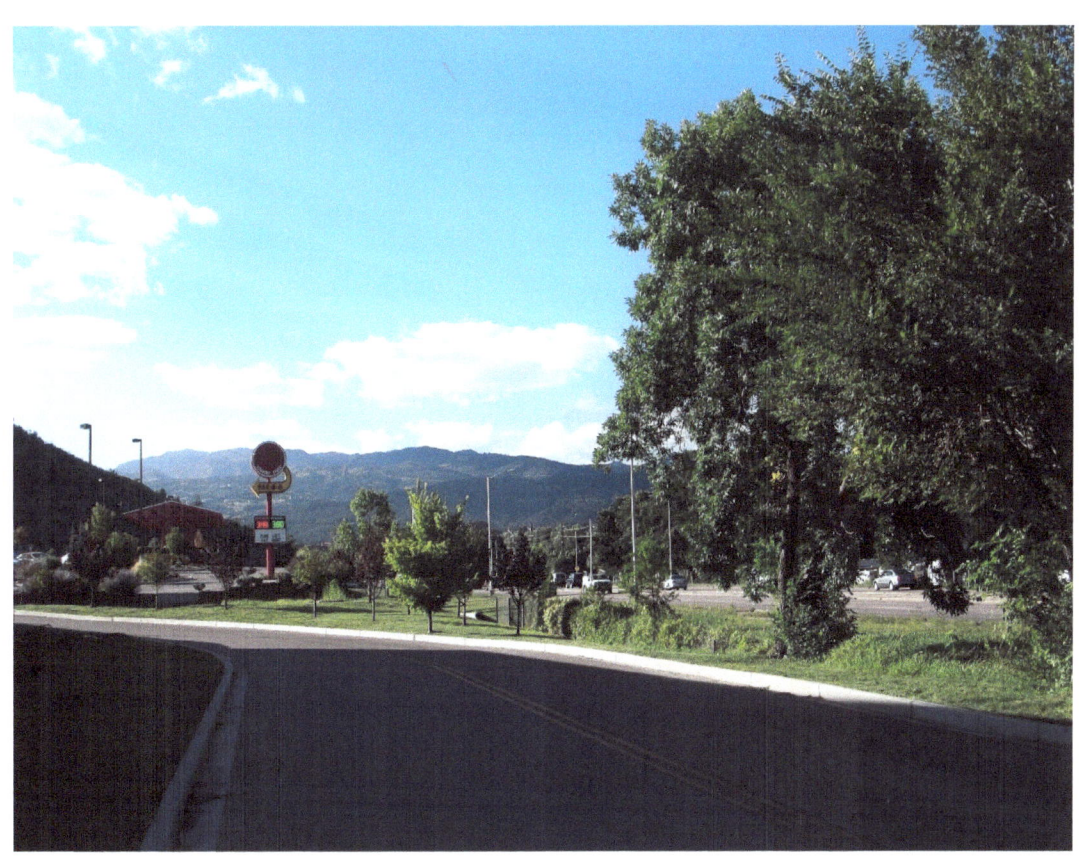

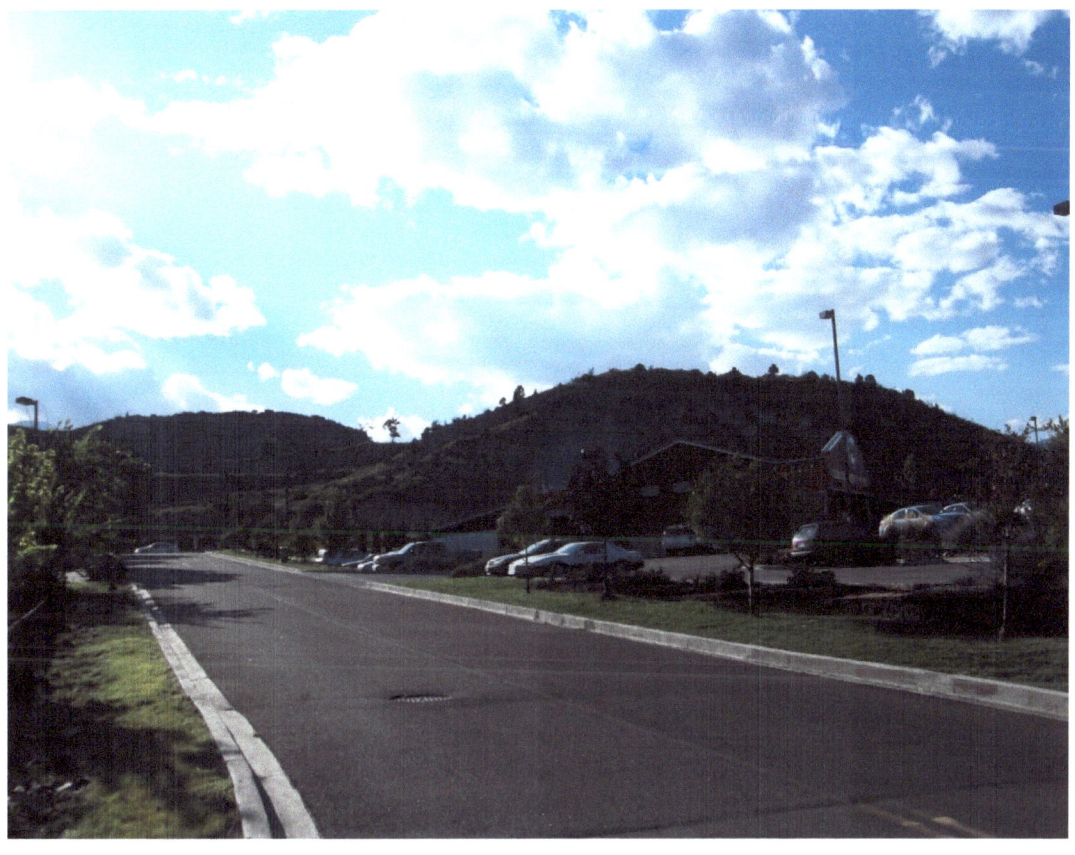

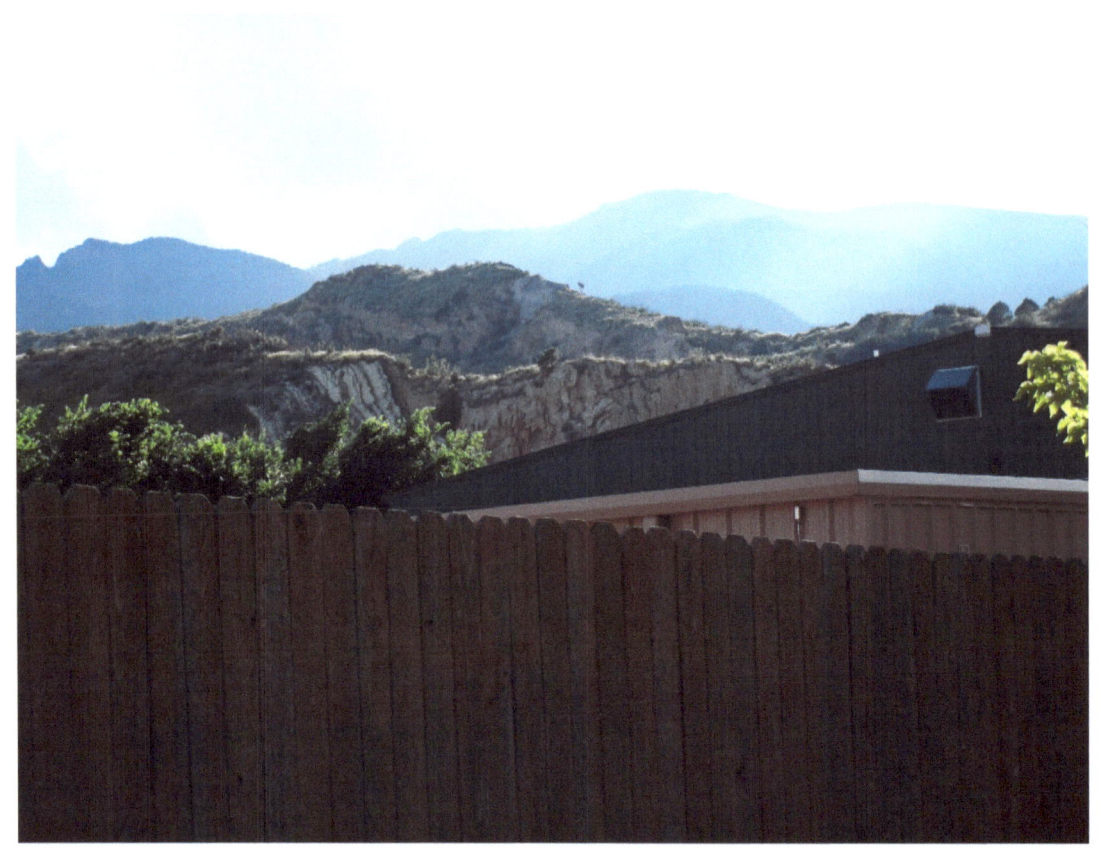

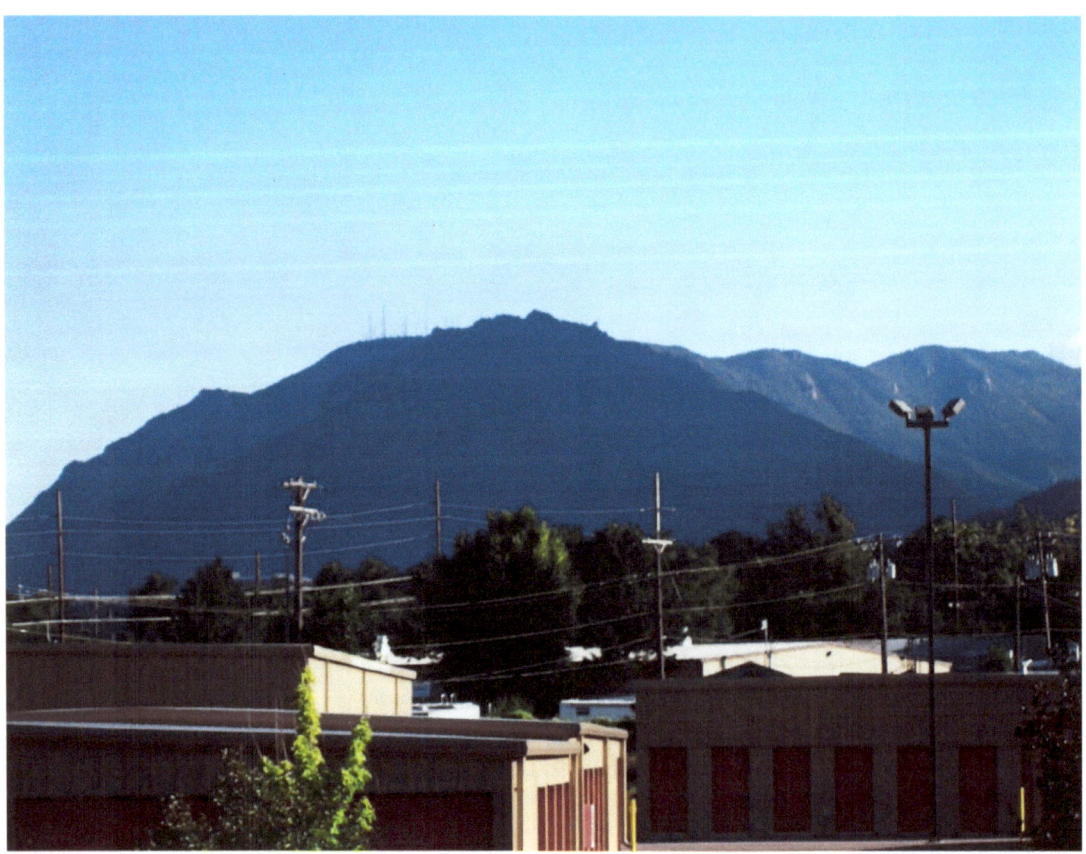

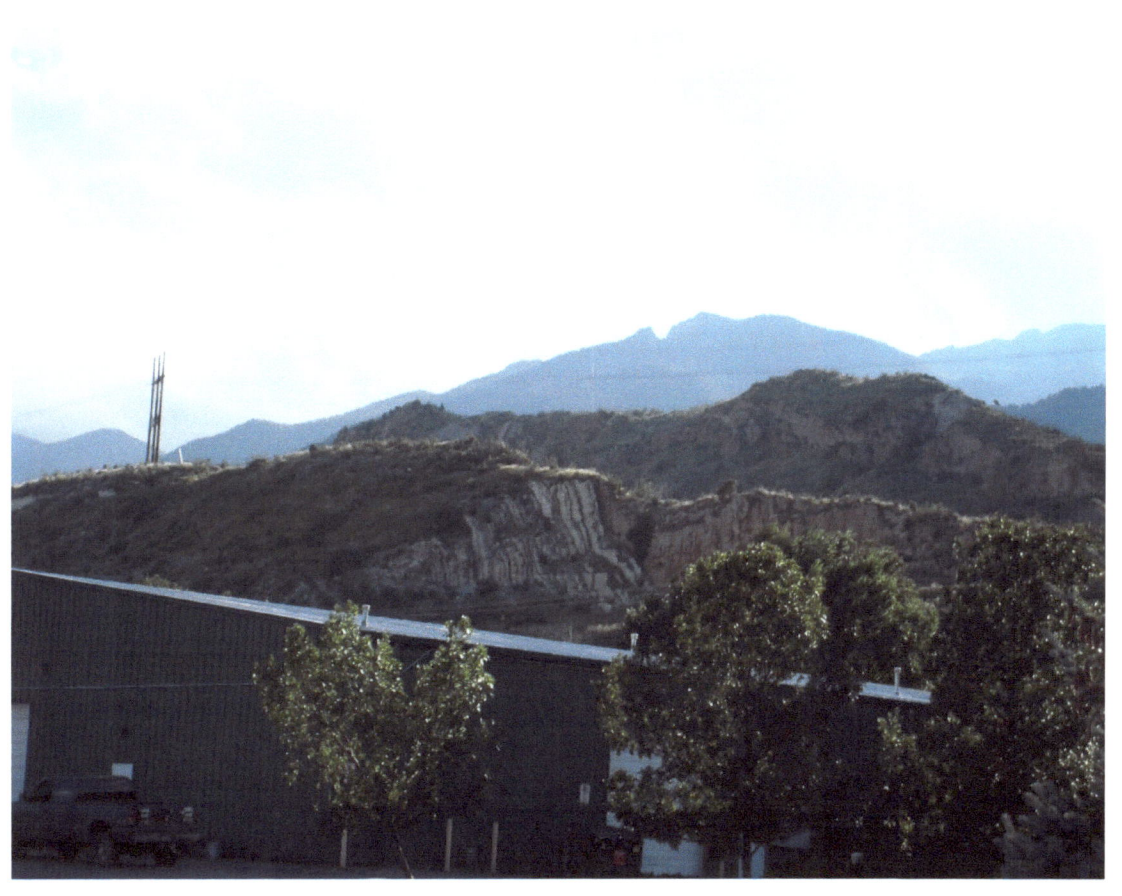

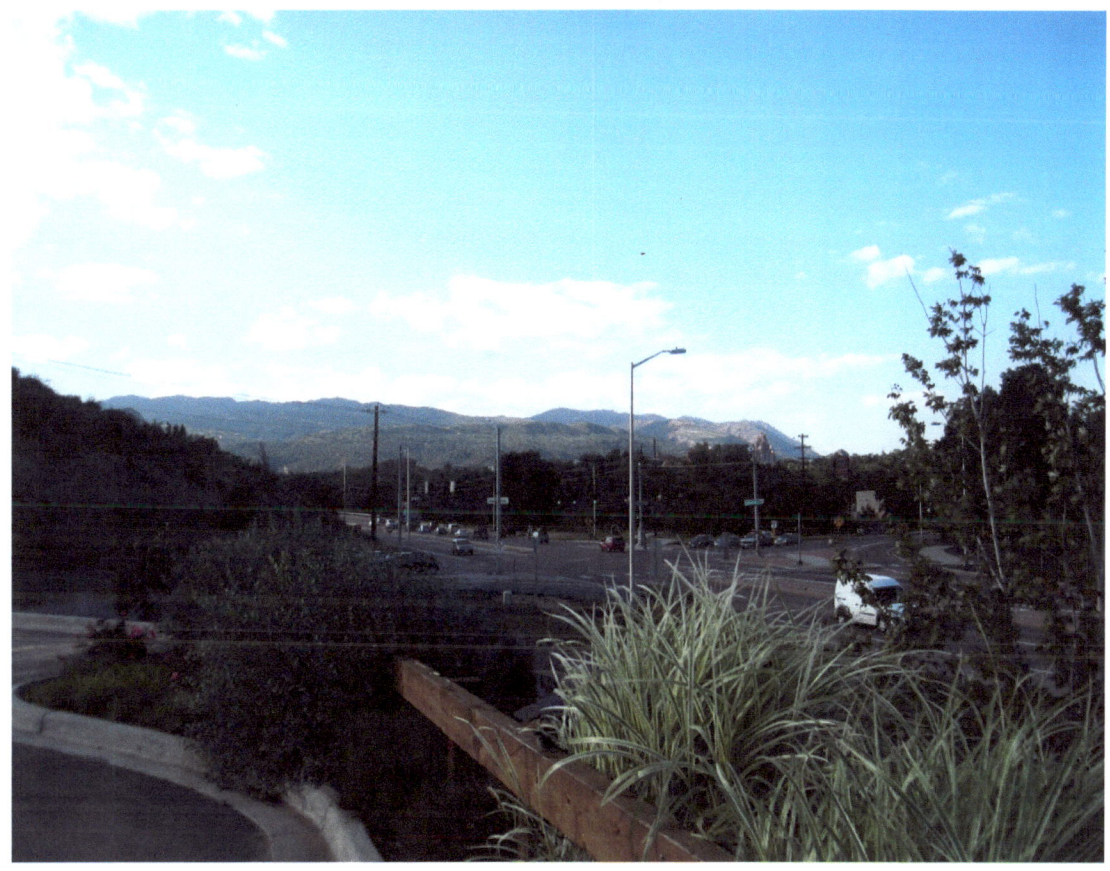

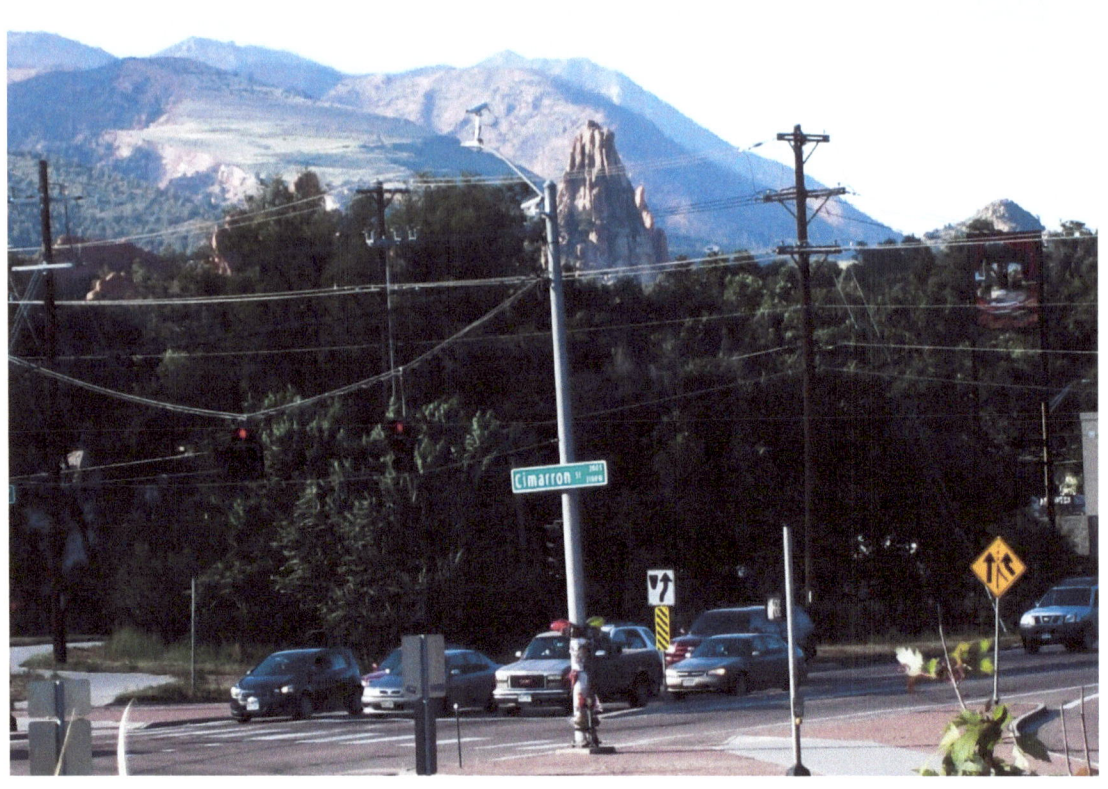

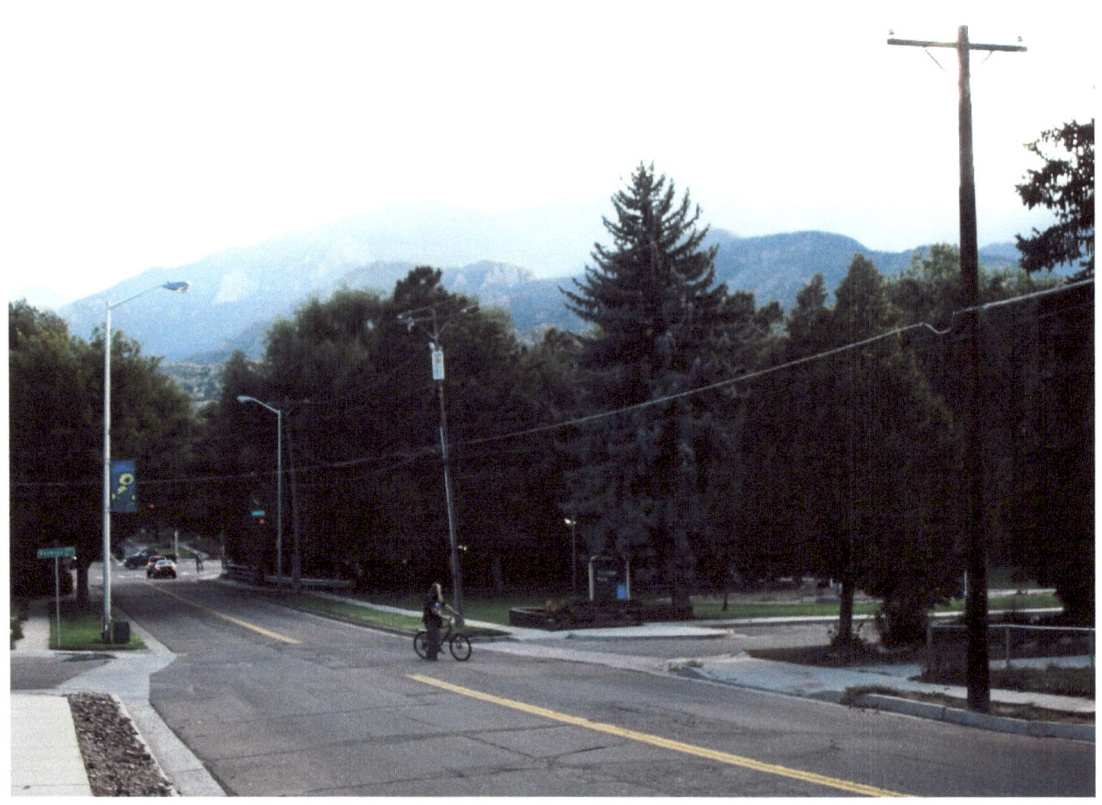

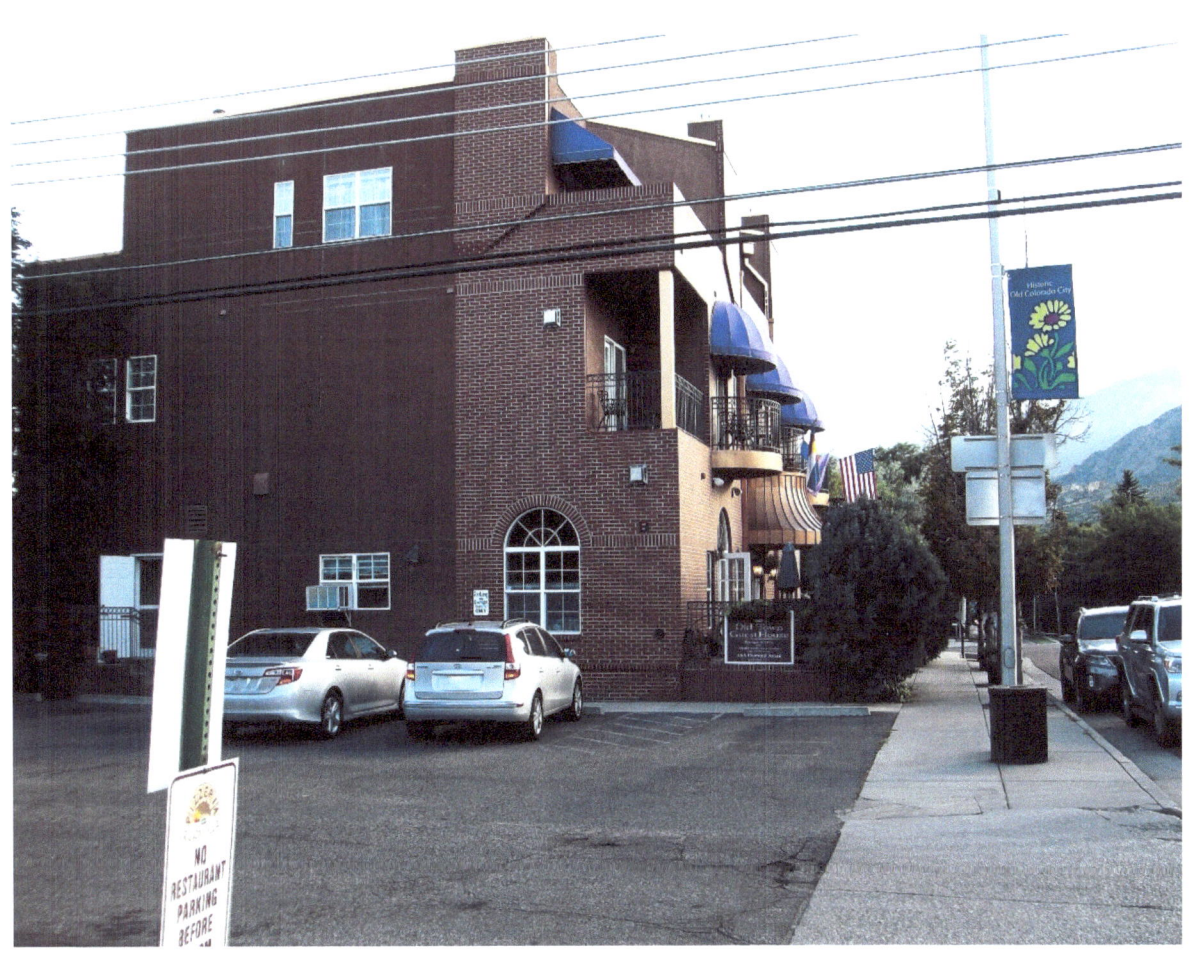

About the Author

Michael Robert Serovey, MA, MISM (1958 - present) is a veteran of the US Army, an avid chess player, web site owner, webmaster and Internet marketer who is now venturing into publishing books on Amazon Kindle. Michael also has earned a Bachelor of Arts degree in psychology from the University of South Florida in Tampa, Florida and a Master of Arts degree in guidance and counselling education from USF as well. Michael has earned a Master of Information Systems Management degree from Keller Graduate School of Management.

Michael is also an amateur photographer who enjoys taking and publishing photographs and videos of beautiful places.

You can learn more about Michael Robert Serovey by going here:
http://AuthorMichaelRobertSerovey.com

Other Books by Michael Robert Serovey, MA, MISM

Colorful Colorado, Vol. 1 – Garden of the Gods

Colorful Colorado, Vol. 2 – Red Rocks Open Area

Colorful Colorado, Vol. 3 – Pike's Peak

Colorful Colorado, Vol. 4 – Winter Wonderland

Castle and Palace Picture Book

Bilderbuch der Schlosser und Palaste: German Translation of Castle & Palace Picture Book (German Edition)

Better Thinking for Better Chess

Death, Resurrection and the Afterlife as Found in the Book of Mormon and Other Writings of Joseph Smith, Jr.

La muerte, resurrección y el más allá como se encuentra en el Libro de Mormón y otros escritos de Joseph Smith, Jr. (Spanish Edition)

If you enjoyed this picture book please give it a favorable review on Amazon. This page gives tips on how to post a review on amazon.

http://authormichaelrobertserovey.com/post-book-review-amazon/

Thanks,
Michael Robert Serovey